GW00498825

Blossom Bliss

Lovingly Crafted for Your Ultimate Enjoyment

Hue Harmony Books

This Book Belongs To:

_____

Thank You

We truly appreciate your support and hope you enjoy every page of this coloring book. If you have a moment, we would be grateful if you could leave a review of your experience with our coloring book. Even a very short review will help us a lot! Simply scan the QR code below with your smartphone:

Leave a Review

Get a FREE Coloring Book
We'd love to give you another series of this coloring book for FREE! Just send us an email by scanning the QR code below, and we'll email you the digital copy of another series:

FREE Coloring book

Alternatively, you can send us an email at hueharmonybooks@gmail.com with the subject line "Free Coloring Book." We'd be more than happy to help and would love to hear from you.

Happy coloring,
Hue Harmony Books

Orchids

Orchids, like whispered dreams, unfurl their vibrant petals,
revealing the enchanting secrets held within their delicate embrace,
and grace the world with their otherworldly beauty.

Aster

In the realm of botanical splendor, the Aster holds a celestial secret,
its very name is derived from the ancient Greek word for "star."
Indeed, as its delicate petals radiate from the center, this
enchanting bloom mirrors the stellar beauty of the cosmos, forever
linking the wonders of earth and sky.

Iris

In the realm of mythology, the majestic Iris flower finds its name intertwined with the ancient Greek goddess Iris, a divine messenger who traversed the heavens, bridging the realms of gods and mortals with her radiant, multi-hued wings, echoing the flower's own rich spectrum of colors and its enduring legacy as a symbol of wisdom and divine communication.

Anemone

In the realm of flora, the Anemone flower holds a captivating secret, derived from its very name, which finds its origin in the ancient Greek language. Anemone, or "anemos," signifies "wind," bestowing upon this delicate blossom the enchanting moniker of "windflower" — a testament to its ethereal grace and resilience, as it sways and dances with the gentlest of breezes.

Bluebell

In the hallowed pages of literary lore, the enchanting Bluebell flower has been an emblem of ephemeral beauty and a symbol of everlasting love. Its delicate azure petals, bathed in the dew-kissed light of dawn, have inspired countless poets and artists to capture the essence of its transient splendor, serving as a poignant reminder that even the most fleeting moments of our existence can be imbued with the most profound of meanings.

Camellia

In the world of flowers, where petals sway with grace, the Camellia shares stories of light and shadow, a beautiful tribute to the unwavering strength of nature.

Tulips

Within the vibrant petals of the tulip lies the chronicle of human desire, a fragile testament to the transient nature of fortune's favor.

Morning Glory

As dawn's first light pierces the veil of night, the Morning Glory unfolds its tender embrace, a symphony of hues painting the garden's canvas, reminding us that each day is a blossoming promise, ephemeral yet eternal in the heart's memory.

Daisy

Amidst the verdant meadows, where nature's brush strokes dabble
hues of life, the daisy stands in modest grace - an emblem of purest
innocence, whispering secrets to the amorous breeze and weaving
tales of love and resilience.

Hydrangea

Hydrangeas in the garden of life are like nature's chameleons,
adapting to the whispers of the soil and swaying with a symphony of
shades that sing to the heart's delight.

Snowdrop

The Snowdrop flower, a symbol of hope, has a unique way of blossoming in the cold winter months. This delicate bloom can push through a blanket of snow, adding a touch of beauty and resilience to the frosty landscape.

Geranium

The Geranium flower has a hidden talent; its leaves can be gently rubbed to release a delightful scent, creating a natural and fragrant perfume for both people and gardens to enjoy.

Gerbera

In the world of blossoming flowers, the Gerbera stands out as a
precious gem with a fascinating secret to its vibrant charm. Each
petal glows with the radiance of the sun, but there is more than
meets the eye. The Gerbera employs a phenomenon called
"composite flowering" wherein a single inflorescence is actually an
intricate arrangement of numerous smaller flowers, meticulously
intertwined to create a masterpiece of colorful beauty. This floral
illusion serves as a reminder that even in nature, art can be found
in unexpected places.

Cosmos

This captivating blossom, a symbol of the universe's boundless beauty, has been known to sway and whisper the delicate intricacies of the cosmos' grand design to those who pause to listen.

Peony

This captivating blossom, a symbol of the universe's boundless
beauty, has been known to sway and whisper the delicate intricacies
of the cosmos' grand design to those who pause to listen.

Marigold

The Marigold, a stunning flower, holds a special place in the world of flora as a symbol of unwavering devotion and celestial brilliance. With its vibrant golden and amber hues, it reflects the sun's own magnificence, infusing the earth with a celestial warmth that dances on the petals and casts gentle shadows on the lush landscape.

Pansy

In the language of flowers, pansy is a symbol of remembrance and loving thoughts, which is why it is often used in literature to convey the idea of sentimental longing or affectionate memories. With its velvety petals and delicate hues, the pansy is a flower that speaks to the heart, evoking emotions of tenderness and nostalgia in those who behold its beauty. Whether featured in a poem, a novel, or a painting, the pansy captures the essence of human sentimentality, reminding us of the power of love and the enduring nature of memory.

Lavender

The soft color of lavender flowers was once a representation of feminine qualities such as elegance and charm, and gifting a bunch of these delicate blooms was a way of expressing strong feelings of love and adoration. Presently, the calming fragrance of lavender is still believed to promote relaxation and peacefulness, and as a result, it is cherished by creative individuals like poets and visionaries.

Sweet Pea

The sweet pea has a delicate and fragrant bloom. Its petals, like soft whispers on the breeze, draw us in with their gentle beauty, while its heady aroma lingers in the air like a lover's perfume. From John Keats' ode "To the Indian Pipe" to Emily Bronte's hauntingly beautiful poem "Remembrance," the sweet pea has been immortalized in literature as a symbol of purity, love, and enduring grace. A single stem of sweet peas can evoke memories of a bygone era, a time when life was simpler, and beauty was cherished above all else.

Daffodil

Behold the Daffodil, fair and bright, for it holds within its golden petals a secret power - a power of healing and rejuvenation. This gentle flower, with its trumpet-shaped blooms, has long been cherished for its ability to ease ailments of the body and lift the spirits of the soul.

Zinnia

With petals like the velvet robes of royalty, the Zinnia captivates
the eyes of all who lay their gaze upon it. Its vibrant hues of red,
pink, orange, and yellow radiate with a fiery passion, as if the sun
itself had taken refuge within its delicate petals. Truly, the Zinnia
is a flower fit for a queen!

Lily

The Lily flower, with its pristine white petals and regal stature, has long been regarded as a symbol of purity, innocence, and grace. In ancient Greek mythology, it was believed that the flower sprouted from the milk of Hera, the queen of the gods, and was thus associated with divine femininity and motherhood.

Chrysanthemum

In the language of flowers, the Chrysanthemum represents longevity, joy, and fidelity. This captivating bloom has been praised for centuries in Japanese poetry and art, celebrated as a symbol of the transience of life and the beauty of impermanence.

Sunflower

Behold the mighty Sunflower, whose golden crown reaches for the heavens like a star-seeking sentinel. Each petal, a ray of sunlight imbued with the warmth and radiance of the sun itself.

Poppy

Amidst verdant fields and rolling meadows, the Poppy stands tall
and proud, a scarlet jewel amidst a sea of green. Its petals were soft
as silk, yet bold as fire, fluttering in the gentlest breeze like the
beating of a thousand ruby wings.

Roses

From the passionate red rose to the innocent white, and the mysterious black, the rose has woven its way into the fabric of poetry and literature, serving as a muse to writers and a metaphor for life itself.

Carnation

The Carnation, with its delicate petals of crimson and white, has been a beloved flower in literature for centuries. In Shakespeare's "A Winter's Tale," the character Perdita famously proclaims, "I would I had some flowers o' the spring that might become your time of day," before presenting a bouquet of Carnations to her love interest.

Hyacinth

The Hyacinth flower serves as a powerful symbol of the delicate balance between love and loss, life and death, and the enduring power of nature to heal even the most wounded hearts.

Petunia

The Petunia flower, with its delicate and velvety petals, may seem
unassuming at first glance. Yet, beneath its unpretentious exterior
lies a fascinating secret: it possesses a unique ability to change its
color based on its environment. This chameleon-like quality, akin to
a literary character's ability to adapt and transform, adds to
Petunia's allure, making it a muse for poets and a symbol of
resilience and adaptability in the world of flora.

Crocus

Truly, this little flower is a treasure, imbued with beauty and significance that transcends its modest appearance.

Hibiscus

From the lush tropical gardens of the South Pacific to the windswept cliffs of the Mediterranean, the Hibiscus flower has captivated hearts and minds with its timeless beauty and poetic grace.

Lily of the Valley

The Lily of the Valley represents the return of happiness and is often associated with the month of May, when it is in full bloom, making it a cherished emblem of renewal and rebirth.

Forget-me-not

The Forget-me-not is a symbol of remembrance and true love and has been immortalized in literature and folklore as a symbol of loyalty, faithfulness, and enduring affection.

Buttercup

In the meadow where the sun's rays kissed the earth, a humble
buttercup flower stood proud, its bright yellow petals sparkling like
droplets of gold in the morning light.

Viola

The Viola represents loyalty and devotion. Its delicate petals,
ranging in shades of purple, blue, and white, seem to embody the
very essence of fidelity and constancy.

Cyclamen

The delicate Cyclamen flower, with its enchanting pink petals, has been immortalized in literature as a symbol of both love and sorrow. In Victorian times, it was a common gift to convey the message "I resign myself to you," while in Greek mythology, the Cyclamen was believed to have sprung up from the tears of the sorrowful goddess, Persephone. Its beauty and fragility serve as a reminder that even the most fleeting moments of joy and happiness are worth treasuring.

Hellebore

In the realm of flora, the Hellebore flower reigns as a mysterious and enigmatic figure, shrouded in myth and legend. This beguiling bloom, with its striking petals of pale green or dusky rose, has been prized for centuries for its potent medicinal properties and revered as a harbinger of spring's arrival.

Foxglove

Despite its danger, the Foxglove continues to enchant and beguile all who lay eyes upon it, for its beauty is simply too captivating to resist.

Jasmine

Amidst the sprawling fields of verdant beauty, the Jasmine flower stands out with its delicate petals, exuding an otherworldly fragrance that enraptures the senses. In ancient Arabic poetry, the Jasmine was often referred to as the "perfume of love," a symbol of purity and devotion.

Primrose

The primrose signifies youth, love, and the first timid steps toward a new beginning. This delicate bloom with its pale petals and sweet fragrance has been immortalized in literature as a symbol of hope and promise, inspiring poets and writers alike with its simple yet profound beauty.

Nasturtium

The Nasturtium flower, with its vibrant petals like flames of fire,
has long been admired for its beauty and uniqueness.

Periwinkle

In the world of literature, the periwinkle flower is not just a mere bloom, but a symbol of everlasting love and fidelity. Its delicate petals of blue or purple hold within them the secrets of the heart, and its fragrance whispers of undying devotion. From Shakespeare's "A Midsummer Night's Dream" to Charlotte Bronte's "Jane Eyre," the periwinkle has been used to convey the depth of emotion and the steadfastness of the human spirit. Truly, this unassuming flower is a treasure of the literary world, imbued with meaning and symbolism that continue to captivate the hearts of readers and writers alike.

Gardenia

The Gardenia's fragrance is said to be so potent that it can leave one spellbound, lost in a reverie of sweet-smelling memories. Truly, this flower is a masterpiece of nature, a delicate yet powerful creation that can move the hearts of even the most stoic of beings.

Clematis

It is said that the Clematis, with its enchanting array of colors and shapes, has the power to transport one to a world of pure fantasy and wonder, where the imagination can roam free and the spirit can soar to new heights. Indeed, this majestic flower is a true marvel of nature, a testament to the boundless creativity and endless diversity that surrounds us every day.

Gypsophila

The fragile appearance of this flower conceals its amazing endurance. In fact, this graceful-looking flower can survive even the harshest conditions, including dry deserts and rocky mountain slopes. In the language of flowers, gypsophila is said to symbolize eternal love and fidelity, indicating its resilience and unwavering character. Truly, gypsophila is a floral wonder that captivates the hearts of all who gaze upon its delicate beauty.

Wisteria Vine

The Wisteria Vine, with its cascading blooms of lavender and lilac, holds a mystic allure. In Japanese culture, it is a symbol of love and perseverance, as its woody vines can endure for decades and its flowers bloom even in the harshest of conditions. As it adorns arbors and trellises with its graceful presence, the Wisteria Vine stands as a testament to the enduring beauty of nature.

Passionflower

The passionflower, a delicate and ethereal blossom, holds within its intricate petals a fascinating secret: it was named by Christian missionaries who saw in its unique structure a representation of the passion of Christ. The ten petals and sepals were said to symbolize the ten apostles present at the crucifixion, while the radiating filaments represented the crown of thorns, the three stigmas the nails, and the five anthers the wounds. Thus, this exquisite flower became not only a botanical wonder but also a spiritual symbol of great significance.

Ranunculus

The Ranunculus flower, with its delicate layers of silky petals in vibrant hues of red, pink, and orange, has long been revered in literature as a symbol of both love and danger. In Greek mythology, it is said that the first Ranunculus bloomed from the blood of Adonis, the god of beauty and desire, as a reminder of his tragic death. And in Shakespeare's play "The Winter's Tale," the Ranunculus is mentioned as a flower that is both "bright and dangerous," a fitting description for a blossom with such fierce beauty.

Gladiolus

Gladiolus is a flower of great splendor and symbolic significance. The Gladiolus is said to represent strength, honor, and moral integrity. Its name derives from the Latin word "gladius," meaning sword, and it was named as such due to the sword-like shape of its leaves. Moreover, in ancient Roman times, the Gladiolus was not only admired for its beauty but also used in ceremonial events and as a symbol of the victorious gladiators, who were awarded a gladiolus flower after winning a fight in the arena. Thus, the Gladiolus stands as a testament to the power and resilience of the human spirit, and its beauty continues to captivate and inspire us to this day.

Calla Lily

In Victorian literature, the Calla Lily was often used as a metaphor for the purity and beauty of the female form, and was frequently featured in poems and romantic novels. Today, the Calla Lily continues to inspire poets and writers, who are drawn to its delicate and graceful appearance, as well as its rich cultural significance.

Printed in Great Britain
by Amazon

47809681R00057